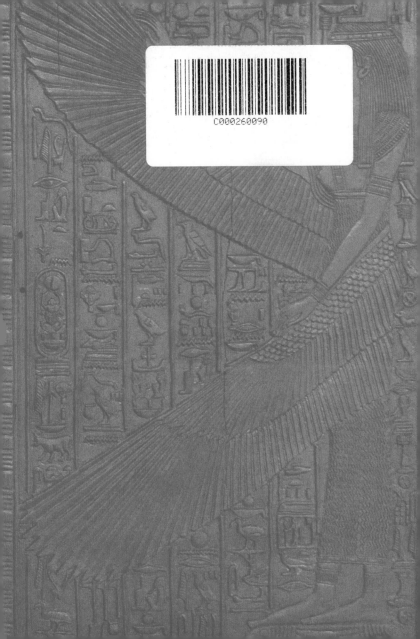

C000260090

THE TREASURES OF TUTANKHAMUN

Introduction by Garry J. Shaw

With 92 illustrations

CONTENTS

PAGE 1 Crook and flail.
PAGE 2 Tutankhamun's inner coffin.
OPPOSITE Ritual figure.

WHO WAS TUTANKHAMUN?

WHO WAS TUTANKHAMUN?

When Howard Carter removed Tutankhamun's golden mask and gazed at the king's face for the first time, the pharaoh had not been seen for over three thousand years. For Carter, this was the culmination of his life's work. A discovery that he knew he'd never match again. For the rest of the world, a new pharaoh joined Ramesses the Great and Cleopatra in their imaginations: King Tut, the Golden Boy. A pharaoh who lived a life of glamour in a time of religious upheaval, and died young. All the ingredients for international fame were there.

And even better, there was treasure.

PREVIOUS PAGES Gold ostrich hunt fan.
OPPOSITE Tutankhamun's gold mask.

Tutankhamun was accompanied into the afterlife with thousands of precious artefacts, so many that it took Carter and his team ten years to carefully remove, photograph and conserve them. Since their discovery in 1922, these ancient treasures have inspired fashion, music, art, movies, TV shows, trinkets and souvenirs. They've travelled the world as the stars of sell-out international exhibitions. The golden mask has become an instantly recognizable symbol of Egypt. A century after his rediscovery, the boy king's celebrity status remains undiminished. Today, everybody knows his name; everybody knows his treasure. But who really was Tutankhamun?

To answer this question, we need to travel back in time to ancient Egypt's New Kingdom, a five-hundred-year period of prosperity, grand monuments and territorial expansion that began around 1550 BC. Early in this phase, nearly two centuries before Tutankhamun's birth, the Egyptian

OPPOSITE Detail of the back of the golden throne: Ankhesenamun anoints Tutankhamun with oil.

army fought a series of campaigns, south in Nubia, and northeast in Syria-Palestine, creating a huge empire. The spoils of war, followed by tribute and tax from defeated areas, flowed into Egypt. The pharaohs praised the gods for granting them success, and in thanks they enlarged the temples – the gods' earthly homes, where divine statues received offerings in dark sanctuaries – and endowed them with donations of land, goods and slaves. When Tutankhamun's probable father, Amenhotep IV, came to the throne around 1360 BC, he inherited a stable country at the peak of its power. Wealthy and unchallenged, Egypt's kings now had unparalleled influence to enact great changes in society if they so desired. Amenhotep took full opportunity.

Within a few years of his coronation, Amenhotep dramatically reformed Egypt. First, he promoted a new state god above all others: Aten, the sun disc. In its honour, he changed his name from Amenhotep (meaning 'Amun-is-Content') to Akhenaten ('He-who-is-Effective-for-the-Aten'), and relegated the traditional gods to unimportance or worse, attacking their names and images. Whether or not this constituted a form of early monotheism is still debated today. Amun-Re, king of the gods, was the target of particular hatred, his name scratched out and erased wherever it was found. And as time passed, other gods faced similar fates, though to a lesser degree. Akhenaten changed Egypt's art too. He had himself – and other royals and nobles – depicted with an elongated face, wide hips, flabby stomachs and breasts. And unlike Egypt's traditional art, which portrayed gods in either animal or human form, or animal-headed with human bodies, the Aten was simply a round disc, its rays ending in hands reaching down towards the ground. At Akhenaten's newly constructed royal city of Akhetaten, today the archaeological site of Tell el-Amarna, Aten temples established worship in the open air because the god needed to be able to touch his offerings.

It was into this Egypt that Tutankhamun – at first called Tutankhaten – was born.

FOLLOWING PAGES Colossal sandstone statue of Akhenaten from Karnak, and the bust of Nefertiti fom Tell el-Amarna.

TUTANKHAMUN'S FAMILY

We know little about Tutankhamun's life before
he became king. Based on DNA studies, he was
probably a son of Akhenaten and one of Akhenaten's
sisters, but the ancient texts say nothing about his
parentage, except that he was a king's son. It was
once thought that one of Akhenaten's minor wives,
Kiya, was his mother, but evidence is hard to come
by. Tutankhamun is not shown on any of Akhenaten's
monuments, where pride of place is given to the
king's six daughters with the famous Queen Nefertiti.
In fact, the only glimpse we have of Tutankhamun's
early life is a scene in the tomb of Maya at Saqqara,
an ancient royal necropolis near today's Cairo.
Maya served as a royal wet nurse, and on one wall
of her tomb had herself depicted with the young
Tutankhamun – shown as a miniature king – seated
on her lap.

When Akhenaten died after seventeen years on
the throne, Tutankhamun was not his immediate
successor. Two other ephemeral kings first held
power, Smenkhkare and Neferneferuaten, though the
order of their succession is unclear. Smenkhkare may

have ruled alongside Akhenaten as co-regent before ascending the throne. His background is obscure, but he was probably Akhenaten's brother or a son, and we know that he married Princess Merytaten, eldest daughter of Akhenaten and Nefertiti. Neferneferuaten was a female king, perhaps Nefertiti herself, ruling alone after the death of her husband, or one of Nefertiti's daughters, such as Merytaten. Whatever happened, and whoever these rulers were, within a few years of Akhenaten's death, the throne had passed to the young Tutankhamun. He cannot have been more than eight or nine years old at the time.

TUTANKHAMUN AS KING

After four years on the throne, Tutankhaten changed his name to Tutankhamun ('Living-Image-of-Amun') – marking a great change by promoting the return of the state god Amun and the return to tradition – and abandoned Amarna for the royal city of Memphis,

FOLLOWING PAGES Ankhesenamun affectionately attends to a seated Tutankhamun on the small golden shrine.

near modern Cairo. At some point in these early years, he married Ankhesenamun (originally Ankhesenpaaten), the third daughter of Akhenaten and Nefertiti. The small golden shrine from Tutankhamun's tomb is decorated with touching scenes of the royal couple. The queen passes arrows to the king while they hunt birds; she helps fix Tutankhamun's collar in place; they sail in a boat in the marshes; and Tutankhamun pours liquid into the queen's hands. Ankhesenamun can also be seen standing beside her seated husband on the back-panel of Tutankhamun's golden throne. The couple had no surviving children, though two mummified foetuses, buried in Tutankhamun's tomb, show that Ankhesenamun became pregnant twice.

With the return to religious orthodoxy, Egypt needed to regain the gods' favour. Tutankhamun left a record of his pious acts on a monument known as the Restoration Stele. The temples had fallen into ruin, he says, military campaigns were unsuccessful, and the gods no longer answered prayers. He restored order by commissioning new divine statues and sacred boats to carry them during processions.

He made great donations to the temples and rebuilt their sanctuaries. The erased divine names had to be replaced across Egypt too, and he seems to have particularly wanted to finish the incomplete projects of his grandfather, Amenhotep III. During this time, the Egyptians began to dismantle Akhenaten's monuments, and perhaps began their attacks on this now hated pharaoh's name.

By the New Kingdom, pharaohs were expected to present themselves as great military leaders. Tutankhamun's armies did go to war, but it is unlikely that the king himself led the campaigns. This duty probably fell to General Horemheb, a man who would later become pharaoh. One campaign was launched to retake Qadesh, a city on the Syrian border that had fallen into the hands of the Hittites, an Anatolian people with an expanding empire. Afterwards, Tutankhamun ordered that triumphant battle scenes be carved of Egyptians riding in chariots, their enemies falling beneath them, and of the god Amun

FOLLOWING PAGES The ceremonial cartouche fan and the ostrich hunt fan, with Tutankhamun in his chariot.

receiving tribute. The Egyptians also fought at least one campaign in Nubia, seemingly to halt a rebellion. Diplomacy was important to the pharaohs, too, and we know that Tutankhamun met foreign dignitaries at court, who spoke to him with the help of an interpreter.

TUTANKHAMUN'S DAILY LIFE

Among the splendour of the golden treasures in Tutankhamun's tomb were more mundane items reflecting his daily life. From these, we can imagine that when the king awoke in the morning, his wardrobe overflowed with options. He could choose to wear one of many plain linen tunics, or perhaps his yellow tunic with green and brown stripes, enlivened by bands of flying ducks. His Syrian-style tunic had an *ankh*-shaped collar, elaborately embroidered with geometric patterns and bands of fantastic animals. Others were decorated with sequins and beads. For formal occasions, he might wear a corslet made of semiprecious stones, a diadem, pectorals decorated with images of deities and carry the symbols of kingship, such as his crook and flail.

For footwear, he could choose sandals of leather, wood or papyrus, some embellished with elaborate beadwork and images of Egypt's enemies. Before leaving his bedchamber for the day, he adorned himself with accessories – amulets, earrings and bracelets. His physical appearance mattered too, for the king owned mirrors, a box of shaving equipment, delicate pots for his eye make-up and cosmetic jars, one with a seated lion on its lid. When attending royal audiences, he may have sat in one of the six chairs or thrones found in his tomb, and jotted down his thoughts using his scribal equipment.

Other objects from Tutankhamun's tomb have an even more personal touch. One box contained a lock of hair belonging to Queen Tiye, Tutankhamun's grandmother. An inscription on a reed walking stick records that Tutankhamun himself cut the reed from the ground. Hunting was a popular pastime among Egypt's elite, and it seems that Tutankhamun was no different, for a golden fan, one of eight found in the

FOLLOWING PAGES Ritual figure of the goddess Sekhmet and detail of a pectoral with solar and lunar emblems.

tomb, bears a text saying that Tutankhamun gathered the fan's ostrich feathers when hunting in the desert near Heliopolis. Two of Tutankhamun's chariots appear to have been ridden, perhaps when the king was hunting, and he built a small palace close to the Great Sphinx at Giza, a popular royal hunting ground. Tutankhamun's other entertainments no doubt included the board game *senet*, for a number of game-boards were found in his tomb.

TUTANKHAMUN'S DEATH

Tutankhamun died after ten years on the throne. Estimates of his age at death have varied, but most agree that he was between seventeen and nineteen years of age. Exactly how he died has generated much attention and no clear conclusions. Among the many theories, one suggestion is that he was murdered by a blow to the head, but few now accept this. Scholars have also argued that the boy king suffered from malaria, a bone disorder in his right foot and clubfoot in his left. Days before his death, he appears to have broken his left leg. Taken together, these conditions may have weakened him physically and perhaps contributed to his death. Others have suggested that the king died in a chariot accident. No theory can currently be proved with certainty, so how Tutankhamun died must remain a mystery, for now.

After Tutankhamun's death, the Hittite king Suppiluliuma I received an unexpected letter from a widowed Egyptian queen, thought to be Ankhesenamun. Without a son, and unwilling to marry one of her 'servants', she asked for a prince as a husband. Having investigated the truth of the situation – important, given the strained relationship between the two kingdoms – the Hittite sent one of his sons to Egypt. He died en route, perhaps murdered. Afterwards, Egypt's kingship fell to an elderly courtier named Aye, a man possibly related to the royal family by marriage. Over the course of his career, Aye had led the chariotry and held various positions that gave him close access to the king, and his wife had been nurse to Nefertiti. To assert his right to the kingship, Aye performed the funerary rituals on Tutankhamun's mummy normally reserved

FOLLOWING PAGES Pectoral in the form of a falcon with outstretched wings and a sun disc on its head.

for the crown prince, including the Opening of the Mouth ceremony. He may also have married Ankhesenamun.

TUTANKHAMUN'S TOMB

When the solemn rituals of Tutankhamun's funeral were complete, his mummy was taken to his tomb in the Valley of the Kings. The tomb's small size – just four chambers, reached by a descending corridor – suggests that it was probably originally intended for a favoured courtier, perhaps Aye, and hastily adapted for the king after his unexpected death. There was only time for the artisans to decorate the Burial Chamber with wall paintings that show the royal funeral, Tutankhamun with various deities, and imagery from an underworld book, particularly the sun god's boat and twelve baboons representing the hours of the night. The funerary priests placed Tutankhamun's body inside three nested coffins, the innermost of solid gold, and lowered them into his stone sarcophagus. In turn, the sarcophagus was sealed within four nested gilded shrines, so large they almost filled the chamber. The king's internal organs were preserved in four small golden coffins, placed in a calcite canopic chest within a gilded shrine.

Once the king's body was protected and secure, his other ritual equipment could be arranged throughout the tomb. Ritual figurines wrapped in linen shrouds represented the king on a leopard or holding a harpoon, or gods, such as Atum, Geb, Isis, Ptah, Nephthys and Sekhmet. Other important statuettes were *shabtis* – small figurines inscribed with a spell to magically compel them to perform work on behalf of the king in death. Two large guardian statues stood at the Burial Chamber's entrance, and a shrine surmounted by the jackal god Anubis was placed to protect the Treasury. Wooden model boats magically enabled the king to voyage through the afterlife realm. Shields and weapons, including a dagger of rare meteoric iron, provided protection. There were musical instruments, vessels of faience, glass and pottery, and painted chests stuffed with jewelry. To provide sustenance for the king, the tomb contained food, including bread, duck and chickpeas, and more than thirty complete examples of wine jars, each bearing an ink inscription detailing its origin.

ROBBED AND FORGOTTEN

Shortly after Tutankhamun's burial, thieves twice broke into the tomb and stole some of its treasures. On each occasion, the tomb was duly resealed by security forces. Despite this initial care, over time, sand accumulated over the tomb's entrance, to the extent that 190 years after Tutankhamun's burial, workers excavating the tomb of King Ramesses VI, unaware of its existence, built their huts directly above it. When the Valley of the Kings was abandoned around 1050 BC, the Theban priests moved many of the royal mummies to a hidden location in the nearby cliffs. They wanted to protect them from robbers, but also to 'recycle' their treasures – Egypt's phase of high prosperity was over, and gold and other precious goods were in short supply.

But Tutankhamun, forgotten, was left behind. He lay undisturbed, sealed within his sarcophagus, until the moment when Howard Carter entered his tomb, three millennia later.

OPPOSITE One of Tutankhamun's *shabti* figures.
FOLLOWING PAGES The Valley of the Kings today.

THE
TREASURES
OF THE TOMB

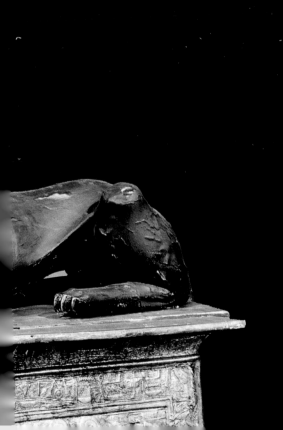

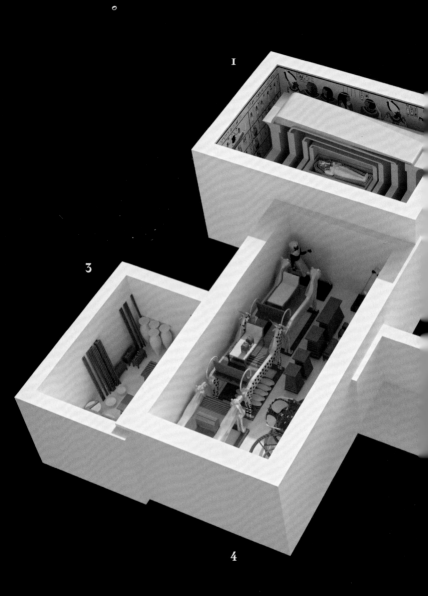

THE TOMB

2

5

6

DAILY LIFE

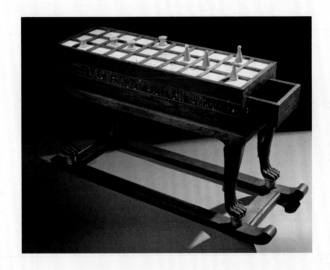

PAGES 38–39 Anubis shrine.
ABOVE Game box with *senet* board.

PECTORAL WITH SOLAR AND LUNAR EMBLEMS

Gold, silver, chalcedony, turquoise, lapis lazuli and other stones, glass
Treasury

Both beautiful and ingenious, this colourful pendant cleverly combines solar and lunar emblems to create a magnificent object full of meaning. In the centre, made of translucent chalcedony, is a scarab beetle, a solar symbol, with spreading inlaid wings and the talons of a vulture. Its front legs hold up a barque carrying the lunar left eye of Horus, itself supporting a crescent moon and a silver disc representing the full moon. Soldered onto the disc are three figures – the king in the centre flanked by the gods Thoth and Re-Horakhty. Completing this fine example of the ancient Egyptian jeweler's art are *uraei* – rearing cobras – and a suspended wreath of poppies, cornflowers and lotus blossoms below.

Among the Egyptian forms of personal adornment such collarettes were perhaps the most prevalent ... According to instructions in the Pyramid texts, the coffin texts of the Middle Kingdom and in the rubric of the 'Book of the Dead' of the New Empire, these collars with their tags were to be placed upon the deceased's neck or on his breast. They were to be of many different kinds, of different materials and of different workmanship – a custom thoroughly illustrated in this burial.

HOWARD CARTER

BROAD COLLAR

Gold, with carnelian and coloured glass inlays
Burial Chamber

In life Tutankhamun would often have worn a
broad collar (*wesekh*) like this around his neck, with
the lotus-shaped counterpoise hanging down the
back to balance its weight. In death it was placed
over the knees of his mummy. Rows of glass beads
are coloured to imitate lapis lazuli, turquoise and
carnelian, while the outer band may represent
poppies. Gold wires threaded through the loops on
the top of the falcon heads held the collar in place.

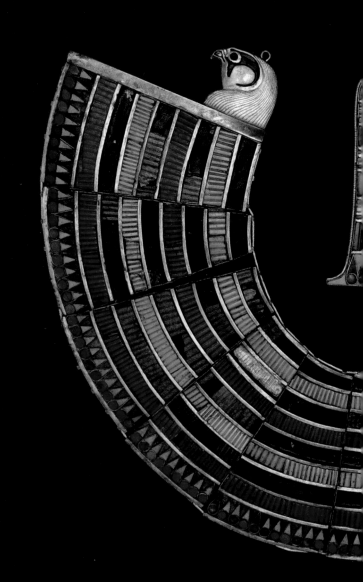

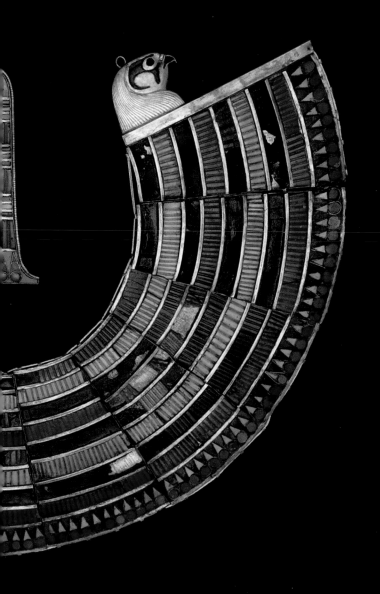

CORSLET

Gold, faience, coloured glass, semiprecious stones
Antechamber

Found by Carter in several pieces scattered around
the floor and in boxes in the Antechamber, this
spectacular corslet is the only known example of
a type of clothing represented frequently in ancient
Egyptian art. An elaborate version of body armour
used for protection in hunting or battle, it was
perhaps worn by the king in official ceremonies,
and would certainly have drawn everyone's attention
to him. It consists of a broad collar joined by the
pectoral at the front to the main band that wrapped
around the body, consisting of individual pieces
of glass representing the *rishi* or feather pattern.
A counterpoise at the back and suspension straps
complete it, though some elements are missing,
probably removed during the tomb robberies.

The corslet as found and reconstructed by Carter.

Corslets of this type are depicted
commonly enough on the monuments,
and were evidently frequently worn,
but we have never before been lucky
enough to find a complete example.

HOWARD CARTER

MIRROR CASE

Wood, gold leaf, silver, glass and semiprecious stones
Treasury

Mirrors in ancient Egypt were usually made of
polished bronze and were highly prized. The one
belonging to Tutankhamun originally kept in this
case may have been of precious metal, perhaps
explaining why it was missing, presumably robbed.
As well as having a practical use when applying
kohl and other make-up, mirrors also had funerary
and religious symbolism. This case is in the shape
of the hieroglyph *ankh*, for 'life', which could also
mean mirror, and is therefore a clever play on words.
Made of two parts, top and bottom, it is carved from
wood and covered in gold leaf, with the interior lined
with thin sheet silver. The decorative inlays in the
centre of the lid form Tutankhamun's throne name,
or prenomen, and the embossed decoration contains
other epithets of the king.

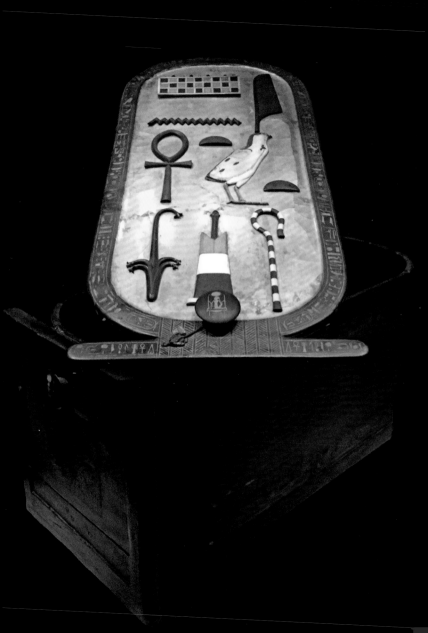

CARTOUCHE-SHAPED BOX

Wood, gilding, ebony, ivory
Treasury

This ingenious wooden box takes the form of a cartouche, the symbolic representation of an oval loop of rope knotted at the bottom which enclosed some of a ruler's royal titles. In this case, finely carved hieroglyphs made from ebony and tinted ivory spell out the king's birth name or nomen, 'Tutankhamun, ruler of Upper Egyptian Heliopolis'. Engraved inscriptions on the lid and sides give other titles and epithets of the king. Even though the box had been broken open by robbers, it still contained important pieces of regalia and jewelry, including the heart scarab belonging to a pectoral found elsewhere in the tomb (p. 107).

We found between the third and fourth (innermost) shrines ceremonial bows and arrows, and with them a pair of the gorgeous flabella – the insignia of princes, fans so prominent in scenes where kings are depicted, carried by inferior officers behind their chief. Beautiful specimens they were ...

HOWARD CARTER

CARTOUCHE FAN

Wood, gold, coloured glass, calcite
Burial Chamber

Several fans of different types were found in
Tutankhamun's tomb, two of which lay close to the
king in the Burial Chamber. One had a head, or
palm, covered in gold and decorated with scenes of
the king hunting ostriches from a chariot (pages 6–7
and 23). The other had a head covered in sheet gold
inlaid with cartouches enclosing the birth and throne
names of the king, with protective vultures either
side wearing the crowns of Upper and Lower Egypt.
Its long handle, or stock, made of ebony, allowed
an attendant to waft it over the king's head to keep
him cool. Originally ostrich feathers would have
been inserted around the semicircular heads, traces
of which were found. An unusual fan discovered
in a box in the Treasury still retained its feathers.
Made of ivory, this fan would have been held in
the hand, perhaps by the king himself.

272

COSMETIC JAR

Calcite, ivory, gold, copper
Burial Chamber

Numerous calcite vessels were found in
Tutankhamun's tomb, which would once have held
oils, cosmetics and aromatic fats. Such substances
were extremely valuable and most had been removed
by robbers, though this jar still contained some
residues. The painted decoration on the body depicts
dogs and lions attacking animals, and a lion is
carved lying on top, its lolling ivory tongue painted
red. The jar's feet take the form of four traditional
enemies of Egypt.

Upon the bowl are the prenomen
and nomen of the king, and
the legend around the rim reads:

May he live, Horus, 'Strong Bull fair
of births', the Two Goddesses 'Beautiful
of ordinances, quelling the Two Lands',
Horus of Gold 'Wearing the diadems and
propitiating the Gods', The King of Upper
and Lower Egypt, Lord of the Two Lands,
Neb.Kheperu.Re, granted life.

Live thy Ka, and mayst thou spend
millions of years, thou lover of Thebes,
sitting with thy face to the north wind,
and thy eyes beholding felicity.

HOWARD CARTER

LOTUS CHALICE

Calcite
Antechamber

Also known as the 'Wishing Cup', this elegant drinking chalice was found lying on the floor in the doorway of the Antechamber, perhaps dropped there by robbers. The bowl is in the form of an opened flower of the white lotus, and the handles its unopened buds. On top of each handle, Heh, the god of a million years, sits on a basket holding a notched palm branch with an *ankh* sign and a tadpole beneath. This whole arrangement, along with the carved inscriptions highlighted in blue around the rim, served as a wish for the king's eternal reign in the afterlife.

A most remarkable and fragile object ...
carved of semi-translucent alabaster,
engraved and painted with chaplets of fruit
and flowers, as if to figure at a banquet
or celebration of some kind. There is
something extremely fanciful about it, as
well as interesting, for is it not but another
glimpse into the faded past breaking forth
from the gloom of the tomb?

HOWARD CARTER

CALCITE BOAT

Calcite, gold, ivory, inlays
Annexe

This unusual object takes the form of an ornamental boat mounted on a rectangular box or tank, all carved from calcite with details picked out in gold, coloured glass and paint. The prow and stern of the ornate boat are carved as ibex heads, and seated at the front, next to the central pavilion, is a naked servant girl holding a lotus flower carved from ivory. Steering the boat at the rear is another naked servant girl. The object's purpose is unknown, though Howard Carter thought that it was an ornamental 'centre-piece', perhaps for a lavish banquet or celebration.

HEADREST WITH BES

Ivory, gold
Annexe

The ancient Egyptians slept with their heads supported on headrests, with linen pads as pillows for comfort. Usually such headrests took the form of a waisted pillar set on a wide flat base, with a curved upper surface to cradle the head. This inventive example is a reduced-size version of a folding stool, with the fearsome faces of Bes decorating the sides. Bes was a protective deity of the household, so would have warded off any danger as Tutankhamun slept.

STICK WITH CAPTIVES

Wood, gilding, ebony, ivory, glass
Antechamber

A large number of sticks, staves and staffs were found in Tutankhamun's tomb, around 130 of them in a great variety of forms and materials, leading to speculation that the king was frail, or, as Carter suggested, that he collected them. In ancient Egypt sticks had many different functions, ranging from walking sticks to those used in fighting and sport and for killing snakes, while others were part of the royal regalia. A group of four, found together, had handles in the form of captives, which Tutankhamun would perhaps have grasped in his hand, thus subduing them. The most complex had curved figures of a bound Asiatic and Nubian, one with details in ivory and the other in ebony. Tutankhamun's sticks show little signs of wear, suggesting that he did not need them for support.

The painted wooden chest at the feet
of one of the guardian statues.

PAINTED WOODEN CHEST

Wood, gesso, paint
Antechamber

Of all the many boxes and chests found in the tomb,
this is the most magnificent. It is covered on the
long sides and lid with paintings showing the king
in furious action in his chariot, either charging
down the traditional enemies of Egypt or hunting
dangerous wild animals in the desert. The paintings
are remarkably detailed, showing enemies falling in
a jumbled mass beneath the hooves of the triumphant
king's horses and struck by the arrows he unleashes.
Inside the box were clothes and robes, some
child-sized, sandals and a headrest.

GAMES BOX

Wood, ivory
Annexe

Like many Egyptians, Tutankhamun must have enjoyed playing board games, and to ensure he could continue the pastime in the afterlife he had game boards placed with him in his tomb. This game box, with a drawer for the playing pieces and a stand with legs ending in feline feet, had its upper and lower surfaces marked out for two different games. One of them, *senet*, a game of thirty squares, was very popular. Players threw knucklebones or sticks to determine how many squares they could move their pieces, with the aim of removing them all before their opponent did. Some squares were marked as being either good or bad luck and the game also had funerary symbolism – a player had to win to ensure rebirth in the afterlife.

ROYAL LIFE

Head of a leopard of gilded wood.

HEAD OF A LEOPARD

Wood, gilding, glass, crystal, bronze
Antechamber

Egyptian priests wore leopard-skin robes to officiate
at important ceremonies, including funerary rites,
and remains of such garments were found in
Tutankhamun's tomb. Imitation robes were also
buried with the king, and two small leopard heads
made from gilded wood with inlaid decoration
may once have adorned them. On the forehead
of the larger one (p. 83) is a cartouche containing
the hieroglyphs for Tutankhamun's throne name:
Nebkheperure.

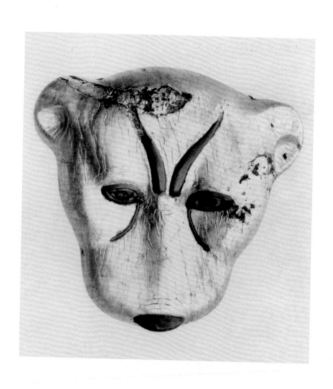

Leopard head made from gilded wood,
perhaps an appliqué for a priest's robe.

DIADEM

Gold, semiprecious stones, glass
Burial Chamber

Beneath his golden mask, Tutankhamun's
mummified head was covered with a beaded skull
cap, on top of which was placed this magnificent
diadem of gold and semiprecious stones. It would
have been an important element of the royal regalia.
The headband fitted neatly around the king's brow,
while the *uraeus* (cobra) and vulture had been
removed and placed next to the king's thighs,
perhaps because they would not have fitted under
the mask. The serpentine body of the cobra stretching
over the top of the king's head would have held the
whole ensemble in place.

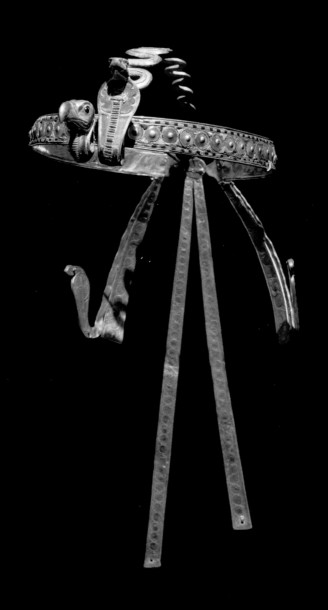

GOLDEN SANDALS

Gold
Burial Chamber

Numerous pairs of sandals of various materials
were found throughout the tomb – some practical
and probably worn in life, others more ceremonial.
This pair was probably made specifically for the
funeral for the king's use in the afterlife, and was
found still on his feet. Made of solid gold, they are
modelled on real sandals, with the soles ridged to
imitate rush or papyrus and the tips turned upwards.

CROOK AND FLAIL

Wood, gold, carnelian, glass
Treasury

Symbols of royal authority, the crook and flail are often shown being held by an Egyptian king, as for instance on Tutankhamun's coffins and mummy. They were regarded as attributes of deities, including Osiris, god of the netherworld. As well as this full-sized set, the tomb also contained a small crook and flail, suitable for a child, as Tutankhamun was when he ascended the throne aged around nine.

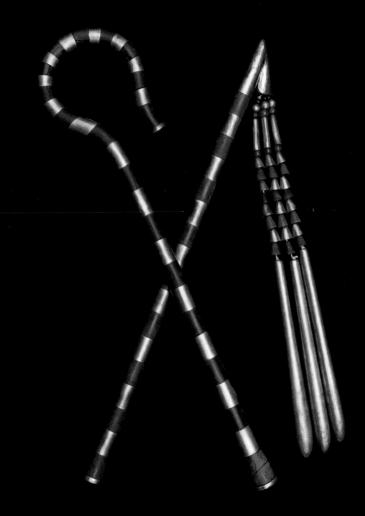

STATE CHARIOT

Wood, gesso, gilding, glass, leather
Antechamber

Tutankhamun is shown fighting and hunting from his chariot on the painted wooden chest (p. 77) and the golden fan (p. 23). He expertly controls the speeding vehicle with the reins wrapped round his waist while wielding his bow. A total of six chariots were found in his tomb, which had first to be dismantled in order to fit through the narrow spaces. Egyptian chariots were light, fast and highly manoeuvrable. They generally had a D-shaped body, open at the back, with a long pole to which a pair of horses was yoked. The 'state chariot' was probably for ceremonial occasions when the king would parade in front of his subjects, dazzling in the sun. The decoration included the king's names and titles, and also images of his defeated enemies.

OPPOSITE A jumble of disassembled chariot parts as discovered in the Antechamber.

GOLDEN THRONE

Wood, gold, silver, coloured glass, carnelian, faience
Antechamber

This magnificent and lavishly decorated golden throne was found rather carelessly tucked under one of the ritual couches in the Antechamber, covered in a linen cloth and with its footstool on top. As well as being a splendid example of royal furniture, which Tutankhamun may actually have held court from, it is also interesting for what it reveals about his life. The intimate scene on the back panel shows Tutankhamun being anointed with oil by his wife, Ankhesenamun. Above them is the disc of the sun, the Aten, with its rays reaching down towards them. The names of the king and queen have been altered, and are given in their earlier, Amarna, forms on the back. The throne may therefore date from early in Tutankhamun's reign, before he restored the worship of the traditional gods after his father Akhenaten's dramatic religious reforms.

It was the panel of the back, however,
that was the chief glory of the throne, and
I have no hesitation in claiming for it that
it is the most beautiful thing that has yet
been found in Egypt.

HOWARD CARTER

OPPOSITE Cartouche on the arm of the throne, containing
the earlier name of the king, Tutankhaten.
FOLLOWING PAGES Rearing cobras with sun discs
on the back of the throne.

Khepre, the scarab, is a transformation of the Sun-god in the form of the famous dung-beetle ... It was in this form that the newly born sun issued from the 'Cavern of Dawn' to begin his diurnal career.

HOWARD CARTER

PENDANT WITH ROYAL PRENOMEN

Gold, lapis lazuli, turquoise, carnelian, coloured glass
Treasury

A row of caskets and boxes found in the Treasury had been opened and some of their contents removed by the robbers. Even so, numerous pieces of exquisite jewelry remained, including this pendant made of gold set with inlays of semiprecious stones and brightly coloured glass. The whole piece forms Tutankhamun's throne name or prenomen – Nebkheperure. The central scarab, *kheper* (made plural, *kheperu*, by the three strokes beneath) stands on a basket, *neb*, and holds up the sun disc, Re.

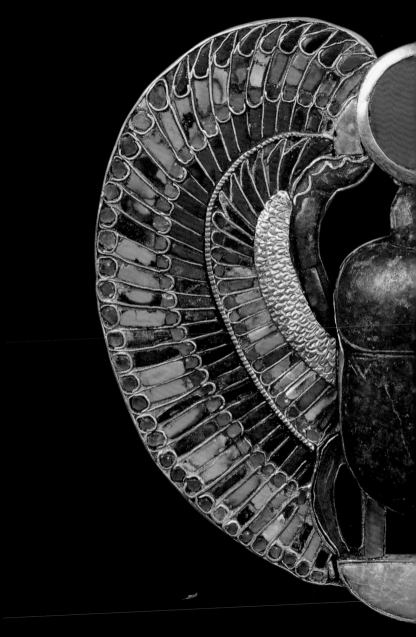

Scarab of gold and blue glass,
with the king standing between two gods.

PECTORAL WITH WINGED SCARAB

Gold, feldspar, carnelian, coloured glass
Treasury

In addition to being an outstanding piece of jewelry,
this elaborate pectoral with a winged scarab is
interesting for several reasons. When it was found
in the Anubis shrine (p. 173), the central scarab,
carved from a hard green stone, was missing.
This was discovered inside the cartouche-shaped
box, also in the Treasury (p. 57). It is a heart scarab,
which would usually be placed inside the wrappings
of the mummy, close to the king's heart, so it is a
mystery why it was not there. The back is inscribed
with Spell 30B of the Book of the Dead, which relates
to the crucial Weighing of the Heart ceremony.
The goddesses Isis and Nephthys support the
winged scarab in the centre of the pectoral. In life
the king might have worn elaborate items of jewelry
such as this during grand royal ceremonies or
religious rituals.

SMALL GOLDEN SHRINE

Wood, gesso, gold, silver
Antechamber

Perhaps originally intended to contain a small statue of the king or a god, this exquisite object takes the form of a miniature shrine with doors fastened by tiny gold bolts. But it is the decoration covering the exterior that is most fascinating and revealing. A series of scenes show Tutankhamun and Ankhesenamun in various intimate and informal settings, including hunting and offering gifts and food to each other.

RITUAL FIGURE

Wood, gilding, coloured glass, bronze
Treasury

A number of objects in Tutankhamun's tomb were not originally made for him, it seems, including this ritual figure found among others representing the king and various netherworld gods contained in a row of twenty-two wooden shrines in the Treasury. Here he is shown as the King of Upper Egypt, wearing the tall White Crown, with a broad collar around his shoulders, wearing a kilt and holding a crook and flail. The face does not resemble other representations of Tutankhamun and the style reveals strong Amarna influence in the soft contours and slightly swelling breasts and stomach. A painted inscription gives the king's throne name, so the figure was intended to represent him in his tomb.

DAGGER AND SHEATH

Gold, glass, semiprecious stones
Burial Chamber

Tucked into the girdle wrapped around the waist of
Tutankhamun's mummy, this solid gold dagger in its
sheath can only have been for ceremonial purposes.
The sheath is decorated with scenes of animals
hunting and the dagger's handle is beautifully
adorned with granulation and coloured inlays.
A second dagger had a blade of iron, a metal that
was extremely rare in Egypt at the time.

WOODEN MANNEQUIN

Wood, gesso, paint
Antechamber

An enigmatic object, this life-size figure modelled as a portrait of Tutankhamun has caused a lot of debate about its true function. Carter thought it was for trying out the fit of the king's clothes, but it may have had a ritual purpose. The arms are cut off below the shoulders and it ends at the hips, and it is possible, as some have suggested, that other parts were joined separately, though there are no signs of attachment if so. The king's large eyes give him a youthful appearance, and he wears an unusual flat headdress or crown, with a rearing cobra, the *uraeus*, carved and painted on the front.

... a little farther along, peering out from behind the overturned body of a chariot, a statue of peculiar form, cut sharp off at waist and elbows. This was exactly life-size, and its body was painted white in evident imitation of a shirt; there can be very little doubt that it represents a mannequin, to which the king's robes, and possibly his collars, could be fitted.

HOWARD CARTER

116

DEATH AND
THE AFTERLIFE

GUARDIAN FIGURE

Painted and gilded wood, bronze, obsidian, limestone
Antechamber

When Carter entered the Antechamber, the wall
on the right, relatively free of objects, was plastered
and stamped with seal impressions – the blocked
entrance to the Burial Chamber. Standing guard on
either side were two very similar, life-size statues.
They represent Tutankhamun, striding with one leg
forward, holding a staff and mace and wearing a kilt
with an apron and a broad collar around his neck.
In one statue the king wears the *nemes* headdress, as
shown on his golden mask, and in the other the *khat*,
or bag headdress. The statues are very striking, with
the flesh painted black, the colour of regeneration;
details are picked out in bright gilding and the eyes
are inlaid with limestone and obsidian.

WALL PAINTING

Plaster, paint
Burial Chamber

The Burial Chamber is the only part of the tomb to be decorated. All four walls were painted with images in tempera on a bright yellow ground. The scenes are intended to be read from right to left, beginning on the east wall, with the king's funeral, where the royal mummy in a shrine is dragged on a sled by a group of nobles. On the north wall is the important scene of Aye, Tutankhamun's successor, performing the Opening of the Mouth ceremony, and the dead king with his *ka*, or life force. The west wall is divided into boxes and represents an extract from the Book of What Is in the Underworld, while the south wall, which was damaged when Carter broke through into the chamber, shows the king with Hathor, Anubis and Isis. Together the scenes are intended to ensure the successful rebirth of the king in the afterlife.

In the centre of the north wall
Tut.ankh.Amen, wearing a wig, fillet and
white kilt, stands before the goddess Nut,
'Lady of Heaven, Mistress of the Gods',
who gives 'health and life to his nostril'.
The third scene, at the west end of
the wall, refers to the king's spiritual
rather than his bodily form: it shows
Tut.ankh.Amen followed by his 'Ka'
(spirit) embracing Osiris ...

HOWARD CARTER

There was a flotilla of model craft ...
Among these craft we find models to follow
the voyage of the sun; canoes for hunting the
hippopotamus and fowling in the Hereafter,
symbolizing the mythical pastimes of Horus
in the marshes; vessels for the holy pilgrimage
to and from Abydos; and craft to render
the deceased independent of the favours
of the 'celestial ferrymen' to reach the 'fields of
the blessed', that are surrounded by seething
waters difficult to traverse ... here, by the
mythical potency inherent in these models,
the king is rendered independent.

HOWARD CARTER

MODEL BOAT WITH RIGGING AND SAIL

Painted wood, linen
Treasury

Boats were an essential means of transport in ancient Egypt. The Nile was a main route for travel, reflected in the fact that the sun god Re daily sailed across the sky in his solar barque. Boats were also an important feature in the royal funeral as they ferried the body across the river from the land of the living to the land of the dead. Model boats are found among royal funerary equipment from the earliest times. A total of thirty-five were found in Tutankhamun's tomb, representing both ordinary craft and large royal boats, as here, equipped with sails, a central cabin and open pavilions at either end. This vessel would have been steered by the broad oars at the stern, topped by representations of human heads.

RITUAL COUCHES IN THE FORM OF A COW AND A LION

Calcite, ivory, gold, copper
Antechamber

Three magnificent ritual couches made of gessoed and gilded wood were found in the Antechamber. Their function is uncertain, but they may have been used in the mummification process or the funeral. The side sections take the form of divine animals, with elongated bodies, one of which was a cow with the sun disc between its horns – the goddess Mehet-weret. The other creatures represented were a lion goddess, Isis-Mehtet, and the hippopotamus-headed goddess Ammut.

Gradually the scene grew clearer,
and we could pick out individual objects.
First ... were three great couches, their sides
carved in the form of monstrous animals,
curiously attenuated in body ... but with heads
of startling realism. Uncanny beasts enough
to look upon at any time: seen as we saw them,
their brilliant gilded surfaces picked out
of the darkness by our electric torch ...
their heads throwing grotesque distorted
shadows on the wall behind them,
they were almost terrifying.

HOWARD CARTER

STANDARD WITH GEMEHSU FALCON

Wood, gesso, gilding, obsidian, glass, silver, bronze
Treasury

This gilded wooden ritual figure of a falcon deity
was found inside a shrine in the Treasury, still with
a linen scarf wrapped around it. On its back is the
royal flail and a broad collar is shown on its chest.
The glittering eyes are inlaid with obsidian, while
the facial markings are of blue glass. Hieroglyphs
painted on the standard's base read 'the Osiris
Nebkheperure, true of voice, beloved of Gemehsu'.

At this point of our undertaking
we realized that it would now be possible,
by opening these further doors, to solve
the secret the shrines had so jealously
guarded throughout the centuries ...
With suppressed excitement I carefully
cut the cord, removed that precious seal,
drew back the bolts, and opened the
doors, when a fourth shrine was revealed,
similar in design and even more brilliant
in workmanship than the last ... What was
beneath and what did that fourth shrine
contain? With intense excitement
I drew back the bolts of the last
and unsealed doors; they slowly
swung open.

HOWARD CARTER

FOURTH GOLDEN SHRINE

Wood, gilding
Burial Chamber

The Burial Chamber was almost entirely taken up
with a series of four massive golden shrines, one
inside the other, at the heart of which lay the stone
sarcophagus containing the three golden coffins
holding the king's mummy. The king was thus
enclosed in a series of magical protective layers.
Howard Carter opened the shrines one by one,
until he faced the fourth, innermost, shrine. Like the
others, it was made from separate pieces and had
been assembled in the chamber itself, and was a very
tight fit around the sarcophagus. Relief decoration
covers its walls – the wooden elements were
coated in gesso, which was then carved and gilded.
The decoration consists of funerary texts and deities,
including Isis and her sister Nephthys on the door
panels, with their wings outstretched, to ensure
the king's safety in the afterlife.

It was a moment as anxious as exciting. The lid came up fairly readily, revealing a second magnificent anthropoid coffin, covered with a thin gossamer linen sheet, darkened and much decayed. Upon this linen shroud were lying floral garlands, composed of olive and willow leaves, petals of the blue lotus and cornflowers ... Underneath this covering, in places, glimpses could be obtained of rich multicoloured glass decoration encrusted upon the fine gold-work of the coffin.

HOWARD CARTER

SECOND COFFIN

Gilded wood, glass, semiprecious stones, faience
Burial Chamber

Within Tutankhamun's first, outer coffin, lay the second, made of wood covered in gold foil and decorated with coloured inlays. It had been covered in a linen shroud, with floral garlands placed on top. The king wears the *nemes* headdress and holds the crook and flail, symbols of divine kingship, in his crossed arms. However, Tutankhamun may not have been the original intended owner of this coffin, as it has been proposed that the face differs markedly from that of the other two. The body, both top and bottom, was inlaid in brightly coloured glass in the pattern known as *rishi*, which imitated feathers, like Tutankhamun's corslet (p. 50).

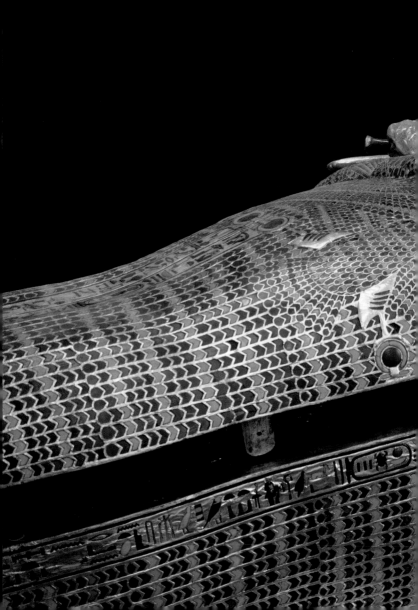

INNER COFFIN

Gold, glass, semiprecious stones, obsidian
Burial Chamber

Tutankhamun's mummified body lay in the innermost coffin, which was beaten from solid gold. Inlaid decoration around the shoulders and arms depicts the goddesses Wadjit and Nekhbet wrapping their wings protectively around the king. As with the other coffins, Tutankhamun holds the crook and flail in his crossed arms and has the vulture and the cobra on his forehead and two necklaces around his throat. The eyes appear strangely black because the calcite representing the whites of the eyes has decayed, leaving the dark obsidian. When Carter uncovered the coffin it was coated in a thick layer of black resinous substance except for the face and hands.

This revealed a third coffin which, like its predecessors, was Osiride in form, but the main details of workmanship were hidden by a close-fitting reddish-coloured linen shroud. The burnished gold face was bare; placed over the neck and breast was an elaborate bead and floral collarette ... I then removed the floral collarette and linen coverings. An astounding fact was disclosed. This third coffin ... was made of solid gold!

HOWARD CARTER

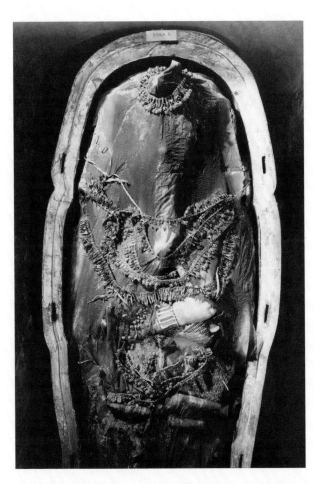

The second coffin opened, as Carter discovered it.

The face of Tutankhamun's first, outer, coffin.

Three thousand years and more had elapsed since men's eyes had gazed into that golden coffin ... Before us, occupying the whole of the interior ... was an impressive, neat and carefully made mummy, over which had been poured anointing unguents ... The beaten gold mask, a beautiful and unique specimen of ancient portraiture, bears a sad but calm expression suggestive of youth overtaken prematurely by death. Upon its forehead, wrought in massive gold, were the royal insignia.

HOWARD CARTER

GOLD MASK

Gold, semiprecious stones, faience, glass
Burial Chamber

Made from two sheets of solid gold hammered together, this breathtaking gold mask covered the head and shoulders of Tutankhamun's mummy. It is an idealized portrait of the king, showing him as Osiris, wearing the *nemes* headdress with the stripes inlaid with blue glass in imitation of lapis lazuli, and the vulture and *uraeus* cobra on his brow. The ears were pierced but the holes were then covered. As with the three coffins, a false divine beard is attached to his chin, its plaits inlaid with faience. In addition to being a beautiful object, the mask served as magical protection for the king's body in the afterlife.

The back of Tutankhamun's gold mask depicts the cloth of the *nemes* headdress, with its blue stripes, gathered together into a pigtail. The shoulders of the mask are inscribed with columns of hieroglyphs forming a magical text from Chapter 151 of the Book of the Dead. This served to protect the king's body so that it would remain whole and functional in the afterlife. The texts associate different elements of the mask with particular deities, such as 'your forehead is Anubis'.

SERVANT FIGURINES

Faience, wood, stone, gold leaf
Treasury, Annexe, Antechamber

In the afterlife, the deceased might be called upon to carry out agricultural activities in the Field of Reeds. To avoid having to do this themselves, the dead were provided with servant figures, *shabtis*, who would perform the tasks on their behalf. Tutankhamun was well provided with such helpers – his tomb contained 413 *shabtis* in a great variety of sizes, materials and styles. It is thought that there were 365 ordinary workers, one for each day of the year, 36 overseers for the 10-day weeks and 12 overseers for the months. These little figurines are usually mummiform, furnished with the necessary tools and inscribed with a spell from the Book of the Dead.

CANOPIC SHRINE

Gilded wood
Treasury

During the mummification process, the liver, lungs, stomach and intestines were removed from the deceased, embalmed separately and placed in four containers, the canopic jars. The arrangement for Tutankhamun's internal organs was particularly elaborate and magnificent. Perhaps because there was no room in the Burial Chamber, the canopic shrine stood in the Treasury, guarded by Anubis (p. 173). The shrine itself, made of gilded wood decorated in relief, was enclosed within an outer canopy on a sledge. Standing on the sledge on each of the four sides were elegant figurines of the four goddesses who guarded the king's viscera, their arms outstretched protectively. One of these, Selket, is shown with her scorpion attribute on her head.

The next in sequence of the
arrangement of objects in this little
room, and also the most effective,
was the Canopic equipment –
a monument not easily forgotten
... Even though it was possible
to guess the purport of this
monument, its simple grandeur, the
calm which seemed to accompany
the four little gracious statuettes that
guarded it, produced a mystery
and appeal to the imagination that
would be difficult to describe.

HOWARD CARTER

CANOPIC CHEST

Calcite, painted
Treasury

The canopic chest for storing Tutankhamun's embalmed viscera was carved from a single piece of calcite (Egyptian alabaster), divided into four sections internally. Individual cylindrical compartments for the four canopic coffinettes were topped by a human-headed stopper, possibly depicting Tutankhamun himself, wearing the *nemes* headdress. The facial features are finely carved, with eyes and brows outlined in dark paint and lips highlighted in red. The sloping lid of the chest and its slightly inclined sides meant that the whole object took the form of a shrine, placed on a gilded sledge.

Immediately in front of the entrance lay the figure of the jackal god Anubis, upon his shrine, swathed in linen cloth, and resting upon a portable sled.

HOWARD CARTER

ANUBIS SHRINE

Painted and gilded wood, silver, quartz, calcite, obsidian
Treasury

Anubis was the god of mummification and guide to the netherworld. This imposing representation of the jackal god, carved from wood thinly coated with gesso and painted black, stood watch over Tutankhamun's canopic shrine. The eyes and brows are outlined with gold and the claws are individually made of silver. The whole object is in fact a carrying shrine, on top of which sat Anubis. The box was divided into compartments containing an assortment of objects, including some jewelry.

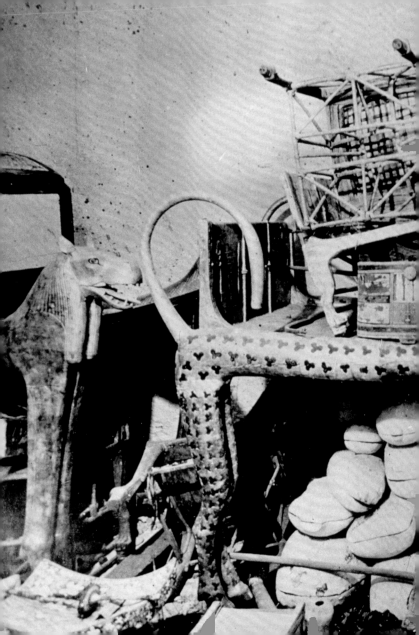

THE REDISCOVERY

THE REDISCOVERY

Born in 1874, Howard Carter had worked in Egypt since he was seventeen years old. He began his career as a draughtsman and excavator, gaining experience before becoming an inspector for the Egyptian Department of Antiquities, a position he held until his resignation in 1905. Two years later, he was hired to oversee archaeological fieldwork projects for George Herbert, Lord Carnarvon. Their search for the tomb of Tutankhamun began in 1917, but years passed with little to show. Although Carter insisted that Tutankhamun's tomb was still there, hidden in the Valley of the Kings, earlier archaeologists had declared that nothing remained of the boy king's burial, beyond some simple artefacts discovered in a pit in 1907. Perhaps they'd been right all along?

PREVIOUS PAGES Harry Burton's photograph of the Antechamber as first seen, crammed with objects.
OPPOSITE Howard Carter and Arthur Mace removing the blocking to the Burial Chamber.

With a heavy heart, in 1922, Lord Carnarvon decided to end his funding. But Carter convinced him to finance one final excavation season – there was a small area near the tomb of Ramesses VI that lay untouched, and Carter wanted to focus his investigation there. On 4 November 1922, only four days into the dig season, Carter's team uncovered a step. They continued to excavate, revealing twelve more steps, and then the upper part of a sealed doorway – a good sign that whatever lay beyond remained undisturbed. That night, Carter sent a message to Lord Carnarvon in England – he had found a tomb, he wrote, 'congratulations'. Despite his excitement, Carter now had to be patient. All work had to stop until Lord Carnarvon's arrival, over two weeks later.

When Lord Carnarvon and his daughter, Lady Evelyn, arrived in Luxor to join him, Carter was finally free to finish excavating the doorway. To their delight, they quickly discovered seal impressions stamped on its surface bearing Tutankhamun's name. Their years of searching had not been in vain: it was the boy king's burial. Soon after, they breached the doorway. They emptied the rubble-filled corridor beyond. It led to another sealed doorway. There were signs of ancient break-ins and re-closings. Would anything remain inside?

On 26 November 1922, they got their answer.

At around 4 p.m., Carter forced a hole in the second doorway. After allowing the hot air to escape from within, he held his candle inside. His eyes adjusted to the dim, flickering light cast in the darkness beyond. Shapes appeared before him. Piles of ancient and beautiful objects. 'Can you see anything?' asked Lord Carnarvon, anxiously.

Carter's reply is almost as famous as the treasures themselves: 'Yes, wonderful things.'

FOLLOWING PAGES Detail of one of the gilded shrines enclosing the burial of Tutankhamun.

Great-grandparents   **Grandparents**

Yuya

Tiye

Tjuya

Tuthmosis IV

Amenhotep III

Mutemwiya

'The Younger Lady'

Tutankhamun

Akhenaten

Ankhesenamun

Nefertiti

KING LIST
NEW KINGDOM, 18TH DYNASTY, 1550–1319 BC

Ahmose	1550–1525 BC
Amenhotep I	1525–1504 BC
Tuthmosis I	1504–1492 BC
Tuthmosis II	1492–1479 BC
Tuthmosis III	1479–1425 BC
Hatshepsut	1473–1458 BC
Amenhotep II	1427–1401 BC
Tuthmosis IV	1401–1391 BC
Amenhotep III	1391–1353 BC
Amenhotep IV/Akhenaten	1353–1335 BC
Neferneferuaten	???
Smenkhkare	1335–1333 BC
Tutankhamun	1333–1323 BC
Ay	1323–1319 BC

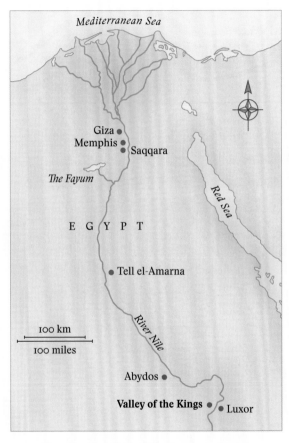

Map of ancient Egypt, showing the main sites
relating to Tutankhamun.

Further Reading

Aldred, C., *Tutankhamun: Craftsmanship in Gold in the Reign of the King* (New York, 1979)

Brier, B., *The Murder of Tutankhamun* (London, 1998)

Carter, H. (with A. C. Mace), *The Tomb of Tut.ankh.Amen*, 3 vols (London and New York, 1923–33)

Dodson, A., *Amarna Sunrise* (Cairo and London, 2014)

Dodson, A., *Amarna Sunset* (Cairo and London, 2009)

Dodson, A. and D. Hilton, *The Complete Royal Families of Ancient Egypt* (London and New York/Cairo, 2010)

Eaton-Krauss, M., *The Sarcophagus in the Tomb of Tutankhamun* (Oxford, 1993)

Eaton-Krauss, M. and E. Graefe, *The Small Golden Shrine from the Tomb of Tutankhamun* (Oxford, 1985)

Edwards, I. E. S., *Tutankhamun's Jewelry* (New York, 1976)

Freed, R., Y. Markowitz and S. D'Auria, *Pharaohs of the Sun* (Boston and London, 1991)

Hawass, Z., *The Lost Tombs of Thebes: Life in Paradise* (London and New York, 2019)

Hawass, Z., *King Tutankhamun: The Treasures of the Tomb* (London, 2018)

Hawass, Z., *Tutankhamun and the Golden Age of the Pharaohs* (Washington, DC, 2005)

James, T. G. H., *Tutankhamun: The Eternal Splendour of the Boy Pharaoh* (Vercelli, 2007)

Kemp, B. J., *The City of Akhenaten and Nefertiti: Amarna and Its People* (London and New York/Cairo, 2013)

Malek, J., *Tutankhamun: Egyptology's Greatest Discovery* (London, 2018)

Naunton, C., *Egyptologists' Notebooks* (London, 2020)

Naunton, C., *Searching for the Lost Tombs of Egypt* (London and New York, 2018)

Reeves, N., *Akhenaten: Egypt's False Prophet* (London and New York, 2019)

Reeves, N., *The Complete Tutankhamun* (London and New York/Cairo, 1990)

Reeves, N. and R. H. Wilkinson, *The Complete Valley of the Kings* (London and New York/Cairo, 2008)

Reeves, N. and J. H. Taylor, *Howard Carter before Tutankhamun* (London and New York, 1996)

Shaw, G. J., *Egyptian Mythology: A Traveller's Guide from Aswan to Alexandria* (London and New York, 2021)

Shaw, G. J., *The Egyptian Myths: A Guide to the Ancient Gods and Legends* (London and New York, 2013)

Shaw, G. J., *The Pharaoh: Life at Court and on Campaign* (London and New York, 2012)

Vannini, S. *King Tut: The Journey through the Underworld* (Cologne, 2018)

Sources of Illustrations

a = above, **b** = below, **l** = left, **c** = centre, **r** = right

Index

On the cover: front and back views of Tutankhamun's
gold death mask. Photo akg-images/K. Scholz (front);
Photo Nariman El-Mofty/AP/Shutterstock (back).

Published in 2021 in the United Kingdom by
Thames & Hudson Ltd, 181A High Holborn,
London WC1V 7QX

First published in the United States of America
in 2021 by Thames & Hudson Inc., 500 Fifth Avenue,
New York, New York 10110

The Treasures of Tutankhamun © Thames & Hudson Ltd,
London

Introduction by Garry J. Shaw

Edited by Sarah Vernon-Hunt

British Library Cataloguing-in-Publication Data

A catalogue record for this book is available from
the British Library

Library of Congress Control Number 2020940842

ISBN 978-0-500-05218-1

Printed and bound in China
by C & C Offset Printing Co. Ltd

MIX
Paper from
responsible sources
FSC® C008047
www.fsc.org